To David

from an island
in crisis,

John

The Dances of Albion

John Milbank

The Dances of Albion
A Poetic Topography

Shearsman Books

First published in the United Kingdom in 2015 by
Shearsman Books
50 Westons Hill Drive
Emersons Green
BRISTOL
BS16 7DF

Shearsman Books Ltd Registered Office
30–31 St. James Place, Mangotsfield, Bristol BS16 9JB
(this address not for correspondence)

www.shearsman.com

ISBN 978-1-84861-395-9

Contents

For my mother in her ninetieth year

To the West

To the West
of the not-yet dead;
lost attributes
for self-haunting.

Shrunken, unapt,
the timeless one:
the brothers' ancient stocky root;
their Jesse-tree,
more potent than
the later may be, yet

'the tube is hard to fit;
he was always small.' Always?
They are puzzled,
out there in the West,
by late damp apples fall
dismayed.

Not over, not over yet.
They mourn their not now mourning.
The old king's shadow
interferes with his own passing.

As horizontal lines divert
transcendence, for a while.
Mark how
the lark and linnet sing
not yet again,
O matchless, matchless man he

must have been:
young nightingale.

Or are they still deceived?
How are they now,
if he is less?

Orpheus, lost Avalon, the West
of the uncanny interval.
One dreamt last night remembered lands,
awake forgot.
And how can he be still
without their clasp?

It is as if they see the spirit itself quail;
whereas the body once bore
in itself a whole kingdom.

But was he always lame
while they still ran?
So may they now outrun him.

Since a new beginning
the one body is always
borne to lie for healing
suspended

in a far-off water
of mist
and orchard.

Dorset Song

Between the seen and unseen danger
twilight falls
to lull us down the cliff-tops' milky-ways.
It makes us float.

Four elements, drifting
within the same medium:
air of the angels
all around us now
kneeling, swooping.

Far-off, to tantalise us
in the moonlight,
the old ringed
and longed-for hill.

These yearnings outlast
all understandings,

while I climbed between
the gate and the electric wire
and snapped quickly the fallen stone;
noted, running, the re-arranged sarsens,
wondered at the gate, broken,
and by whose hand? Why
the twisted, knotted, newly
turned-around signposts?

To mislead walkers?
As the new
and urban signs
so will command us.

Unlike those allegories of choice:
old white and black
and sweetest pointers;
world ash's human branches,
very paradigm
of upright three dimensions.

Whether to the longed-for,
or the headland seared by sunset to a flying island
as the car-beams laser open to but heal at once
earth's cataracts.

Autumn, still my first love.
At your first breath
Man's fire stirring,
and Man's deed making
every down anew.

Our walks to be a dream
where every step
will sound a symbol
of a landscape really buildings,
over cliffs really creatures,
whose graves the sea ceaselessly
is doomed to disinter.

And our business also
to dig and merely wonder
at the limit, at the outside,
in the outlasting.

Between the lyric
and the hymnic
forever poised.

Over cliffs really creatures,
Giant molehills monuments,
every far-off dream-hill
truly once a dwelling;
rites held out of doors
and swans for farming.

Height to height
and light to light,
like butterflies and minor gods
or aerial photographers
we make this plot,
pretend to view
a former fate

where Hardy's rustics still forgive
what seems to them but nature's lot.
And Darwin claims to read the oldest age.
While our own human time,
time of our first desires,
beginning twilight, is declared
unknown.

Swans for farming,
rites outdoors,
the swinging sign-board:
Royal Oak.
The scrolled-out giant,
sacred well –
an antidote –
the druid-groves
where men must hide
at fall of state,
the heroes' hour.

In carved-out *temenos*
Apollo's light once fell.
And truth dictated deeds of kings
and dread
foreshadowings.

Since, without terror,
truth would have usurped
its own arrival.

So for then truth fell
as the knife in the back,
as the relic shafts –
as signposts of the last
quivering gestures
of human limbs.

Autumn, my first love
and the human risings.

Black-haired, red-lipped,
with the oak, beech,
ash and elder garlands.

First and opening *agon*:
writings, writhings.

Pointings begun
only when ended
with the vanishing of their lies.
Cancelled, fulfilled
with the failure of their calculations.

Ancient speech, its run.
Poetry as memory, law that lay
between the lyric and the hymnic.
In the small churches
(there was less wealth here
than in East Anglia for example)
are still encrypted the
old roses for Lydia, chants for Apollo
newly emergent.

Light to light,
height to height
new-born to smoulder.

Shepherds, shepherds all betray.
Gabriel: half Judas, half
evangelist: St John.

Shepherd, once yourself betrayed,
still lead me as a lamb that is sheltered
from death always
by your exchange
of premature slaughter.

True shepherd, lead me.
Dance the hill-tops, our devisings.
Oldest angel, fly the cliffs that pile
the record of our sins before our time.

Lead me, from the hill-tops to the pastures.
Show me secret hidden bones
and unused openings.
Lead me, shepherd to your death again,

where you alone do not betray,
no longer indicate.

If I escape this wire and gate,
these pagan tramplings, farmers' wiles,
I will pass through Saint Wite's stone wounds
some ring, bangle or other token.

The Children in the
Land of Summer

Treasures not always from darkness.
Treasures once sprung from the light.

To mourn a lost love:
better, longer
than love's pretence.

As dreams
the living dead. Though old and changed
they once desired
town brides for country garlands;

girls who never could abide
were needed
from the nethermost
to be.

Resting with desires and still
not passing eastwards
to the cure of no-desiring,

while trees by shadows skirted ever seek
to touch their ghost
which then would vanish
even beyond nightfall

since, for centuries
we culled our secrets from below,
we paid their price and met the keeper

at the crossroads of the drover's road.
By the gnarled beeches,
by the skirting branches,
at a price he yielded,
though he held the songs, the seeds.

Lessons of darkness:
there was no escape.
We needed ruses
to discover the secrets
of the ruses we would need
again to locate secrets.

In those days, for that man
whose fate was to give;
that very thing
was used against him.

In those days there was no escape
from the three curses:
Lessons of darkness.

Not from the scream heard in every hearth-place.
Not from the listener to every word in the whole island.
Not from the depletion of Hades' cauldron.

Here, uniquely,
came the day of the death of the gods.
When they fled to the barrows,
and when one, without shelter,
captured the forever by a ruse,
naming it but one night
and a single daytime.

Which tumulus is his,
driving westwards
by dorsal roads,
forever Friday?

Intoxicated by ancient swellings
that loom larger than yesterday.
Buried projections
that are most potent to command us.

Our needs are still theirs.
Their gifts for us to give.

And who are these people
and where from, newly stranded?
Arrived without hope of healing.
Where from, the old same dark ones?

Always from seawards and beyond,

since up and down is mapped
on here and there, but here alone.
Here is a there that misses our glimpses:
here of the mist, the sea
that might be island. There
that is also here on dark days –
on most days of the north.

Days when their there and then for them,
is also here and now for us.

To dwell already in the over-there,
where they come from,
where we are yet to go,
is to dwell forever
in the island of the mighty.

Your fate still, my children.
Here in the land of summer,
in the time of apples' fall,
at the season of faint, fast
bright dismay
of fading sun.

Here by the old steam-train,
on a journey that has already been taken.
Paid-for excessively,
paid to the keeper
who dredges up a treasure
from his swelling cave-hoard.

The relic-quest is yours
O children,
whose faces can only be of the past.
Of a legendary time that you visit
freely for a certain price,
when children once roamed here
in the land of summer,
everywhere.

Arabella, you clasp your old doll
as you wave to the driver
with an antique gesture.
Arabella, who has not paid,
You write continuous writhing lines,

shifting the triforium to the horizontal,
dissolving the vertical exchange.

Yet we adults still count the cost.
Again sacrifice is demanded.
Dark stores pile up our pleasures
to a meagre, partial yield.

Sebastian sings:
I show
The deep romantic combes
that thwart the length of hills.
Long, long and spiralled line
Of Quantock, let us pay
no further dues for music.
Let us pray:
O heavenly quire,
let down her scale.
Give us below,
let it spring up
as showerings from above.
Return, return to us a king,
to hand us still along, and teach us till
we sing our way
and free dark lords.

The Pembrokeshire Cosmology

I

Like one among the dead,
confined within the truth
of an unlivable disclosure,

I imagined that in another land
this tangle would have flourished

to bear our orderings
and nurture our assertions.

Since every fantasy
according to Augustine
exists somewhere,
or else the perfect would not be.

And how is being
which is itself one,
not of perfection?

But for now
I am appropriately left
to the land of those begotten
from the god of the dead
(after life, begun)
from across the sea.

In this land I pray
for the gift to imagine
again my truth elsewhere, free.

Though for now to be captured by this freedom,
I stand here in chains, captivated.

And I pray for the gift
to fashion in words this truth
flourishing in the land
from before the dead.

For the gift to praise this land
which is in the one being.

What I wish to receive
is the power to return
the one favour and with this favour
myself to return, always.

II

The prophetic land I find
at first disappointing.

It is a surveyable peninsular:
like a map of itself,
more intellectual.

The body strained through the neck
to a gaunt head
which then detaches
to the bubble-thoughts of islands.

All Europe shrunk,
concentrated,
gradually departed.

By isolation of essence,
entropic equilibrium.

I am caught between the undertow
and the riding of a wave.
Suddenly I am going in the wrong direction
and death not dream has caught me.

Hearing my cry, arms reach out and
I am recaptured by life,
but it is as if from thenceforwards
I am the child of death
brought to a sterile birth,
returned to the iron plateau
as now my homeland.

If here is sacred renewal,
then it is born, in secret,
of a strange desolation

from the top of withered trees
like leaves already dying.

Absolutely blasted by the sea-reared winds,
the plateau is worn down
to the last terrifying
and extraordinary resistance
of the curved hills.

They are like skeletal fins
bonded to the sea:
Carn Lidi, Carn Perfedd, Carn Fflad,
Carn Treliwyd, Carn Leithyr.

Primaeval things are shown here;
the incredibly hard, because incredibly old:
where a black cloud of ravens rose
and a blue cloud of warriors fell.

Suddenly going in the wrong direction.
It is a question of the right people
                in the right places.
Yet all we know for now are journeys.
Dissonances, distances
and ultimate departures.

Between banks of stone and grass,
lone gorse,
black clouds of ravens rise

and vanish.
Whirring chaffinches, like little machines,
are suddenly sprung-born from a gaunt tree.

At evening there are swarms of minute bats.
Tribes of insects; legions of slugs
rendering livid the late-summer dampness.

All is blurred
with the blood of dark hawks,
and strange substances have been smeared
over uncertain horizons.

Walking to the post-box
over the iron plateau,
I survey the reduction of culture
to its essence of prophecy.
The closed shops, meagre produce,
cold façades
and slurry-dumps at the edge of villages.
A comfortless succumbing to *ressentiment*
and mad hopes for a reconquered Britain.

Till that re-enchanting,
from this drained place
there will come no cheer
for them or for me,
alone in the twilight blue joy
over the flat land

where my companions are bent trees,
barbed fences, primaeval telegraphies,
clear-outlined cottages, resting, floating
on the surface of the peninsular

that is nearly a severed head:
removed, like Bran's
in order to survive, alone
in its foreshadowings.

III

With diligence
I nonetheless set out,
since I neither could depart in dreams
nor ascend to an elsewhere,

to seek some signs of its possible past descent,
serving still to me
for meagre prayer.

Prescelly lay, I read
at the crossroads of western ways and waters,
           at the intersection
between Hebrides and Cornwall,
Salisbury Plain and the South of Ireland.
Here apple-trees grew in secret
        in the forest of Celyddon
with their flowers all foxglove pink.

There were crows swooping across;
magpies starting up.
But around the violent borders
are the flowing languages
and eventually
sea and land appeared to mingle.
A strange milky brume
was distilled out of the trespassed horizon.
It yielded a blend both refreshing and tiring,
awakening and yet soporific,
invigorating but dream-inducing
like mother's-milk or sex.

In such an atmosphere
the air turns white and palpable,

while the rock
becomes white and vaporous.

Perhaps one might after all
come here to dream.

And first I sank into the valley of
                    the hiding cathedral,
dedicated to the man of released honey
that he drew from the Queen-bee of monarchs

whom satin and fruit-trees bless;
air and atmosphere.

To the man who lit a fire
all through this valley,
suggesting a more powerful sacrifice.
He was hidden, here in this enclave
for a retreat, safety, subterfuge
and secluded strategy.

As in Prescelly,
the march of the mountains
like bounding steeds
curve a passage for the boar-chase,
so here inversely and identically
he sought the dip and journeys underground
to the cave's mouth by the seashore.

Tunnelling all divine praises,
while the tower rises straight above the choir
as if for birds to sing from the base of a tree
hollowed out to resonate.
Still the chanters peer down from their mossy eyrie

at the forlorn congregation
far further-sunken.

And then I found
a perfect black beetle on the cliff-path,
glossy-black and bulging
like an inkblot evolved to a sign.

This microcosm indicated
the weaving of the same patterns
eternally by gulls, skylarks,
kittiwakes and guillemots,

and by rocks arrested for a moment
in gigantic restlessness, and by small farmsteads.
By the men, even, still walking their woven lands.

Every cliff-face, nearly, was perfect.
I marvelled at the way each outcrop
                fell into a shape
that one could perfectly desire
and scarcely could have
                imagined.

But one alone, in a remote bay,
was fearsome and ugly
like an abandoned quarry once worked by slaves.
Such evidence of demonic intervention
suggested that my habitual vision
of an astonishing maritime order
was no illusion.

Into these exactitudes of nature
persons may not necessarily fit.
I asked of the cliffs

whether when whenever
their forms should come to
be glimpsed by us,
we might perhaps be permitted to add to them
and be unique by fitting in,
to fill them in with detail
beyond even the scope of their repletion.

IV

What was the most beneficial measure
that Adam accomplished?

Who was confessor
to the gracious son of Mary?
And the ebullition of the sea –
how is it not seen?

Rapid curves and plaited chains.
We catch by a strained wisdom
the crucial gaps which we might occupy,
but are confined to the memory of those
who once knew answers.

When there stood Troy-Town,
the original labyrinth;
an exact model
of the entire stellar universe

whence came the new line.
Bringers of life from the dawning sun
like the gypsy-girl
with her red scarf and dangling earrings
whom we sometimes encounter --
so dark, moon-kissed and gaudy
down the damp, pale, western lane,

bringing longing to us from where
we long not to go,

one of Diana's crew: she came
with lingering Brutus.
He who engraved an altar in new Troy,

slew the last giant
and hurled the dragon downwards,

before he dictated
that the eldest son should rule
under the Pendragon,
for the time being,

always, secretly to instil
the usages of Britain:
that a wife, children
and instruments of his calling
might belong to a man.

That Queens may rule
to greater victory.

That the forest,
unworked mine and
hunted creatures
are common to all.

That the child, old
and family instructor
are exempted from all work.

Nor are there weapons against these.

While there is equality of rights
and equity of taxation.

With a mixed government
at once regal and popular.
Without both,
then never to be either

in New Troy of the oak groves,
ringed summits
and branching temples

in all the local sites,
dispersed to yet more centres.
Some places are more than others
and without this priority
there would be neither order nor beauty.

Yet for a place to be a place at all
it must constitute a centre.
Otherwise the detailed and lesser
would be merely the random.

Everywhere disperses to new,
absolute and unique dispositions.
The whole island is
but one great place and centre.
It is as the One,
                Being, Intellect
manifest equally everywhere,
the entire also in the lesser places
and the minor saints.

The island, like Goodness,
is dispersed throughout itself
and overflowing beyond
its elusive circumference.

V

All the traces of a past: glorious,
strange, still arriving, I found there.

All the elements for worship descended,
encircling,
unused like the closed Bethels.

I reflected on the capture
of the most vital places.
On the exile to the head
to flee the corruption
of the heart, bowels and entrails.

London: from whence the head was disjoined
from its nether roots,
betraying the usages of the island.

Cambridge: unfed by sacred milk
and lacking to dull eyes
its own fenland light
at once so gold and misty.

Where giants of ignorance, snobbery and vanity
again now roam,
proferring their style without substance,
cowardice masquerading as modesty,
impotence as discretion:
the creeping credentials
of scholarship as a sterile terminus.

And Oxford: at the island's centre,
unillumined by the self's lord,
trumpeting its dragon reward

for the betrayal of wisdom
to the uniform order.
All amidst glories most abstruse
and extraordinary,
unnameable splendours
and strange, secret by-ways

where evenings are captured
in ancient and deliberate fashion
and gatekeepers still know
to keep guard for something
as yet inaccessible.

All this essential
reduced to mere background,
whereas it announces so much more
than any of its polite denizens.
As if such music were too much
for their ears to hear
and so they constantly sought
to render it plausible
that there was, of course, upon analysis
only silence,
through hour upon hour of solemn tutorial.

VI

Up on the corn plateau
with stones and stars
a bee hums
the first tune of the actual.

There is shelter above battle,
a book in the origin,
a long train of horsemen
treading through a maze
in Julian's bower.

Here at last
I came upon a vision that caused my senses to flow
like liquid dew or
sea-foam surging, melted honey-comb.

In the enchanted realm past concealed doors,

through the white sun of a hundred mergings,

a century's distinctions
can be revealed.

They are the one light
itself altered
to splayed, blanched rays
drawn back
through a blank burning.

I had followed the twisting road
to the far mountain
and the lair of beauty.

To the whiteness near the sea:

the shining sky,
the brilliant shining ray,
the radiant flame,

within the circle of the Sun,
with the child emerging.

Past the long white houses
in the widening of paths,
through fields the colour of light
which disclose the colour of light
as radiant green.

Through fields
like jewels sown together
with spaceless thread.

Down past the pink, perched cottages
after the emerald woods
to the striated rocks
whose surgical incisions recall
the criss-cross geometry
of the dark hedgerows above me,

or else the pattern of a green-black scarf
worn by a woman knowingly,
as an enigma of the erotic,
drawing the male with a fury
beyond all natural explanation.

VII

This dream cannot be known without a book,
as it records so many colours of horses,
armour and equipment,
of precious mantles and powerful stones

in tones of the sky-light,
emanating ray
and burning flame-light.

As the black raven's blood
running on the white snow
reminded him of his true love,

like the black sheep
changed to white
when they crossed the river,

so he gathered the blue stones for her eyes,
the white stones for her skin,
the red stones for her lips,
the black stones for her hair.

And he had never
gathered enough of them.

But at least
he had come upon a store of gifts
to renew his energies.

And by the first buildings in the world,
the first tombs, vaults, lintels,
worked through an exchange
to assert a centre that had always

secretly been there,
within everything like the depth of the surface
of the new sea-green colour painted
but yesterday upon the bedroom wall,

he was consoled to think on every hour
that any hour of the day or night
might bring news of her from any one
of a myriad unknown messengers.

VIII

In the course of my return
I arrived at the castle of a gift-bestowing lord,
where one might ask for shelter
as that would prove further
his already renowned prowess.

It was Raglan,
last headquarters of the West,
where I mourned the library of destroyed Tintern,
lost here to a further and remorseless stalking
of the universal truth.

And a strange calm prevailed
and a strange power of assurance,

when I recalled Peredur
who asked not to be interrupted
while he reflected upon
the one to him dearest,

solemnly aloft for an instance
while journeying in Gwent
that was erstwhile Monmouthshire –

gazed at from my bedroom window
on the other side of Severn.
My father told me that this was neither England nor Wales,
which seemed to my childhood a solemn enigma
as I lay awake on an early summer's night
looking through my curtains in consequence
at pure Britain, only.

Once a transport of blue stones from Prescelly
to an upland body laid bare in its whiteness,
beneath a blue scarf, canopied.

A Jutish Recounting

I awoke in London
to a dream of the sea,
of impossible white cliffs
nonetheless terrifyingly there
by a sudden shore, a surprising
sea of shocking
grey turbulence at the end
of a suburban street,
resuming London at
a granted distance.

Alarmed for defence,
precarious passion of
Thanet's ruptured escarpment,
the exposed white crumble: 'unto
Jesus bid you welcome', with
the steamships looming
before the spectral isle; suffraged
life bent into gargoyled-pastoral
that may be sheer horror, turn by jolt,
rummage and sweep. We
are stark frozen in our stare
out to the snow skies
looming over dark liquidity.

Defence against the demonic
inrush of the sea-wolves. Nature
is what is mourned, where
laws of passion threaten sense.
Codes and tunnels; heart's sweet grave;
the sleeping fortress of the pale island.

We are there waiting with him
buried inside us
within the inward threshold.
Waiting on wonder
already transpired. Already washed
over us as salve
and prophylactic against any
eventual invader.

One should have waited;
one was not to know.
But those are alternative blasphemies.
The passion that ensued on
late-arriving truth
was as perfect as infinity
and most eminently precarious.
We held the enemy at bay in that
moment by suffering
precisely his assault in
our measuring of it. So was
protected the instance of joy. So was
life first lived and resurrected, so it
was pierced through our flesh to
exalt just in knowing our loss,
then to expand eternally
but first in exultant waves
again and again, to Bach's grave lilt,
to his unbearable welcome
of our appropriated saviour. We bid it
and he entered and we began to live
at the moment of our expiry.

Truth in the wind of this justice
along the Kentish coast.
I now foreswear

all later compensation as loss,
donning instead the ritual
of mourning, to offer the upshot,
the first step which proved the last
as we knew
in that very moment and could not desist,
for we had to die
if we were to have commenced existence.

Pinioned to the cliff: the first
and last line of our defence. Jutish
men take up the task
of the British they once ravaged here.
They initially faced the elements
and likewise at the end. It was
for the sake of the interior.
That there might be forever an inward
as Logres, become Mercia become
land-locked Midlands in secured time,
for always unto the finish
where mild swellings of breasts
merge with the wild withstandings
and intrusions of onslaught that
victory itself may merge with calm.

East Anglia

The winds
high up in the rafters with owls,
with angels,
speak of the other, kindred eaves.
Far sentinels of echoes
by the wrecked coastlands.

When you enter their bleached chambers
of salt woodwork
and unutterable height –
voyaging inverted –
you fear the nothing in the end
besides the acid marshes.

But at this safe, Cambridge distance
I imagine, from down in my pew,
a gaunt giant, one-eyed and from
far-rafters' cross bar suspended

nine nights alone
with owls and crumbling angels,
fastened by wooden bolts
and not nothing yet,
this old god, since the fate which binds him
is only evil.

In consequence there *are* things,
held by the wooden rivets of the ship's stern.

The Trent Aegir

Water like a running wound
leaks northwards with
a stealthy rush around
aberrant bends that wind
the roads through shades
of dampest green.

Sleeping dragons coil
beneath the low, mysterious rises,
basking in stranded meadows
of wrought flowers
near the red arks
nestled within or besides
the seeping river.

The stranded manor
is like a vast gouged-out tree-bole,
which reveals in its crocked structure
all the hidden properties of wood
to warm, fire, shield, ennoble,
elevate, enfold and decorate.

Within its shelter
and all along the alienated streets
that recent time has left here and forgotten,
we hear the boom of the countervailing wind
when it meets the southward ninefold rush
of the whelping tide-bore
as the cold northern invasion
penetrates once again
these lands of indecision

between pragmatic pilgrimage
and sensuous abandoned poetry that is wild
with suggestions of lost beauty always strung
along elusive threatened threads
coiling to strange oases and unexpected heights
above the green-bleached bleakness.

Ware Aegir!

The king cannot command reversal of
the alien tide which brought him.
His singers rather blow with the lyrical wind,
to make resound for many a mile
their healing resistance
to the surging of the warring waters.

The Hunting of Bartle

As one to pass through clouds
I turned aside
from the juggernauts –
their taut throttle
of seamless journeys
obliterating in pride
mere occasion of departure,

knowing I had outrun
already the north wind's sources,
but at the back there danced still
rumoured, purer sunlight
about the trees in shapes of ages
never planted
or reflected pale

from rock of bridges, houses –
built of inner-nature to out-nature her
just as discretely
as gleaming, writhing, wondrous streams
forsake their secret chambers,

drawn down, long since,
like Apollo's scions –
with pondered angles, order plighted
now or then
and quite before *will* reaching
by a single silver thread
along the unicursal maze

to flee the beast or lure him:
Holy Bartle,
whose burning saves
because he is the voluntary
victim,
resuming and renewing
unthought nature's style within
the justice due to
the raptor and the overbearing.

Since neighbours do not meet unless
they see in what they love a distance.
So we pass by the perfect fields,
forever there to promise life,
and stones we may not dwell within
but proffer as the
monuments to ended chase.
The thief and giant now the
saint, as one upon Pen Hill
to guard all local lives
in Wensleydale.

Northumbrian Round

Very early,
very early in the world.

The world to be explored as yet unknown
will be found to be quite different
from hitherto.

The early world –
by the long walk at the edge of the moors
in the first light
that assumes evening.

Past the cross at the first crossroads.
The cross protecting in battle,
so that forever after
there are delicate places where one scarcely treads,
that one scarcely pronounces.

And now no longer
but forever in remembrance.
Heavenfield: where is it located?
Lastingham: now so small.

Must the real hero remain unknown?
That his act not be embellished
with the lustre of fame?
Must his real deed be unenticing,
like the long labour of days
without a death-ride?

Then he is unsung
and unreported.

May never have been
for certain knowledge.

So something of glamour
must he also have sought
alongside toil
in order to be remembered.

And his fighting was also this writing
that shuns not the least spectacle.

Very early, very early in the world.
The unknown ground where he fell,
simply struggling, like all the others,
is yet greener and more emerald always,
could we but find it.

Such lustre once saved
the post of a house from burning.
The post endured, not in order
to save the house,
but to let it point forwards,
recorded beyond its own destruction:
the unknown dwelling.

Before battle, in the first light,
already the erected cross
cured an arm for its wielding,
and little fragments, continuously distilled
down the ages in the purest water
mend all of what ails us.

They prepare men, in the final era,
for a good death.
And the Church in its course declining

ever since Eden –
always its towers glimpsed by the traveller
at last, in the late evening –
dies well its own death through
imbibing these small morsels.

And is, in order
to be at all
this same well-dying.

A spectacular secret spectacular heroism
is thereby somehow recharted
in the midst of undignified failure

by a sufficient remnant
who bring back with their sudden
but rehearsed, correctly predicted
and right conjunctions

the first freshest times,
those blowing first steps
and a breezy balm of Tansy.
In running Mead-light,
with the waves like the scrolls of viols
riding in low, ferociously
to greet the golden Bass of the shore-strands.

Better to be sad, lost,
and in the truth, than
feigned-happy for trading.
Since in truth there is being
and the kernel of joy –
your end of the thread
that another will yet find.

Here absence is not oneself alone,
but oneself lost with the other
gone entirely missing,
as tears bear a man outwards
on a high adventure of release
from the pointless journey.

There was space: here is convention.
There was movement: now is confusion.
And there was, will be again
a moved order, of sure dancing.

New acquisitions, and a new, sudden mood.

Three kisses from the Prince of Norway
will disenchant the dragon.
So I dream, through my window, near the bay,
dissolving in glad tears to wind, autumn and ruin;
to decline even unto the sixth age.

When the last, lone, disenchanted princess
stands in her silver castle-turret
at the northern summer-midnight
looking eastwards, over the sea.

Now the transferred Celtic island,
no longer set in sunset,
awaits its full retinue of horses
and the Prince to awaken
or arrive from Norway.

She watches, above humanity
for their singular proud positions
beyond temporary constellations:

Deneb, Vega, Rigel, Bellatrix,
Arcturus, Sirius, Aldebaran, Spica,
Alnath, Mirfah, Dubh, Alioth.

All the legions of justice
which are archetypes:
not to be assigned our roles,
though they possess them.

They are the myriad, watched legions
of the first time,
before men erected the *gnomon,*
and instead launched *azimuths*
to the far horizon
over the green-mounded bones
of the guiding dead
who lilt and lull
the southern landscape.

Etched here northwards
in the whorls and lozenges
of stone depictions.

All the stars of the first time
proclaimed a single invisible light
before the dawn of the Sun –
usurper and blood-seeker,
on the pretext of omens.

And to watch their movements
is to wait in patience
for their widest circle:
when each in the great year
lights the circle of the Zodiac.

Pausing in the Autumn of time,
in the melancholic evening;
kin to the dry and cold earth,
which is our element
according to the *szygia*
of *homo, annus* and *mundus.*

In this time, our time, every time
– since time is a measure
or a fold in the real that risks *fiat*
in order to reach the precision
of marking –

in this final falling-off of days
we may chart, each year, according to Bede,
the failing of winter twilight towards dawn
and not utter blackness.
As though it were a northern summer's night,
never quite occurring.

A summer midnight of the north,
when at the evening of the Sabbath
as it begins to dawn towards the first day

– not towards the night this time,
and so never towards the night,
never from the beginning towards the night

but instead, from the very outset,
from the evening towards the morning.
And from evening to evening
engrossing twilight,
that spectral imagined
of invisible kisses
for sufficient beauty.

At this very darkest hour
which yet proves not absolute,
but only evening,
a merest darkening,

the Princess will greet her silver spans,
returning. While the sun rises
to show modestly to the *dioptrae*
his first step of advancement.

Not the sovereign centre to demand blood,
but bleeding itself of the invisible
amongst the many stars he entirely illuminates
in the path of their remoter light.
The holy angels and heroes
who pass out of shining.

He, the absolute image,
has also his phases
and evenings of remembered
and re-sought assignations.

Once every year, a pace beyond
the tomb of darkening,
if his glamour of arrival
be recorded of the Moon
in her alluring fullness.

And Bede could date
this conjuncture for the future.
He knew the arrangements
for all future assignations,
and here deciphered
the endless returning of the Cosmos

which was for him its being
as first created.

The thistledown is blowing on the moors
and there are white clouds in sympathy with yellow shoots.
Golden fields wheel round imperceptible
to become the golden shores,
and we must cross and re-cross the great north routes,
while the wind meets the sea and the sun strikes the stones
at the intersection of all kingdoms.

The Circhenn Medley

Time
that comes in clusters
soon.
Again is later
when you went away.
The heaving and hirpling
of so many clouds,
will lead us at length
to the sacrifice stone.

Up the hill-fort, to the white walls,
scale the other *Cathertun*.
White and brown, the sloping echoes,
in the older afternoon.

Oh the knight,
the knight of old green mould!
How can he lie so stone and cold,
with more life than is ours?

The swithers of the winding breeze,
the spurtle fine for steering,
The clairted Childe
comes home for good,
his mouth now sealed
by alien blood.

Soft love stole over me that day,
besides the breeze of evening.
The rustle and bluster of trees half-withstood,
between the shot-spume of the waves
and waving of the larches.

Time
that comes in clusters
soon.
Again is later
when you went away.
I dreamt that still with you I stood
besides the scattered *Tormentil.*

The Concealments of Buchan

The sea swims with green
and swarms with silver.
The sun casts its vast
irregular petals over the
shoulders and leas of the headland,
coating with miraculous exactitude
every bump and dip.

Houses are three-dimensional shadows
of invisible time. Arraigned
in wedges of three, side-on to the sea,
as the gaunt spokes
of a rugged primaeval clock.

Their gable-ends offer to the waves
the most possible resilience. In urban
unity to pretend them away, yet
to be with them in the mode of rocks,
purporting no interior, albeit
they secrete multiple electric caves.

The wine tower's rumoured rooms
were found unreachable by stairs,
and the priest's walled-up
tomb in the castle may only
be revealed within a maiden's dreams.
It proves impossible to reach the punished,
self-punished or the mourning lover.

Meanwhile the evening's gloss loses itself
in the silver dawn, parting gift

of the departed moon. To betoken
a spectral day, disclosed by the parted
curtains of summer's faint-drenched darkness.

Out at sea, flocks of gulls hint
at the presence of seals or dolphins,
while of seven sons drowned
one has left a coming heir
to a secret bride who will
eventually be embraced by grief.

Unfindable is the third stone
in the river to be cast out with
the other two if inheritance
is to go smoothly forwards.

Still worse is to follow:
blindness and death,
should the enclosed chamber
ever be opened. On the outer sill
of the tower-window is scored
the name of the abandoned bride,
stowed in another, forsaken room.

Of her death, the new bride and
her descendants can never be innocent.
Nor can we reach the useless wine-stores
and the walled-off sanctum. Nor readily
knock at the doors of the granite
long-houses under the lights of the harbour
that beckon us to other beacons,
far-flung seawards, in an arching chain.

Inland the sudden startle
of king-led starlings in

fanned-out, wing-like ranks
reveals the secret seethings
of the hidden, lost people
not acknowledged by their changeling cousins
who man the post-offices, the drearly
cosseted newsagents, the information
centres or the upturned boats.

Ethereal Banffshire

Air that can only be seen.
Light that angels might breathe.
The land spun so thin
that it must eventually break,
but before then spread unended
to new plains of bleak pasturage,
humming vision into unbearable chill rapture,
faintest haze of life further refined
as harr and then even that strained
through the gauze of invisible wings.

The body gasps and chokes for lack
of solid sustenance or wind
of any savour. Before
the treeless swells that betoken
unimaginable gulfs and ruptures,
slowly the spirit spills out
to meet earth's final distillation,
learning how to live forever foodless,
mythless, at one with the sky,
unrespirate. Doomed to rush out
with the sea's tide to greet
the sun's fall into faintest fire.

The Legacy of Alba

What waters, doubled depths
and self-chained sequences!
Islands shell out to sea
to mosaic light's labyrinth.

Antechambers of antechambers:
God's eye split to a glistening shoal
of endless spread. The golden blood
offered on the stilled tide. With
the victim once erect, already
resuscitated on the vertical altar
between the conical uprights. Fragments
of airy light now solidified
and piled stonily upon each other.
Indifferent mutual clinging. Effectively forever.

Lochs anticipate seas in sanctified
corridors of preparation. Seas insinuate
themselves into land which is cast out
as islands. Thrown forth as nets
to catch the tinctures of the waters.
Heights twist horizontals to spirals,
while trees watch out in darkness
to delay the march of mountains
descended in shadow to the shore and
veiled forth into their own reflections.

Triple suns and four elements:
the dry, the wet, the burning
and the unfelt breath within,
until it hurls one over in
terrible gusts and squalls although

its blows remain invisible.
Of unseen giants that compel
the sudden drenchings and
teasingly-vivid returns of light.

Sentinel curved shadows before the Flow Country.
Visits of trains to stops in the mere mire.
Private crossings and secret telephones
in the ferny strathes. Once a widowed Queen
walked in a stunted garden of brittle beauty,
contemplating escape to the further island
of red rock for a while. The northern coast
defended with perfectly potterised old embattlements.
How unlike the gross whig clutter
of the one same slaughter, both far and near,
the far brought near as conquest, the near
made far in the same death of beast and people,
the old land ended with the spirit's vanishing.

Lush and swathe of wild
for a while, rising to shelter
more intense colours than known to the south.
Restless desire to leave here and to return;
do the journey again and this time
further. Further up the Pictish coast
to see the hidden Hyperborean towns
beginning kingship again behind the wind
after the darkness has already fallen.

With a Davidic twist. Now Constantine
of the north rules with his harp
and words come like music to celebrate
life, but life lives only with these notes,
only with these articulations. Then

the lion is tamed, straight-beaming
from transcendence, from gold beyond the sun,
higher than the morn,
the horse no longer ambulatory,
but its legs so criss-cross, settled, commanding,
here to stay in war with the dogs stuck
within the rood, ready to die,
to end all other pain of the innocent,
ready to rule by dying and die by ruling.

Out of the bounds of the beyond striding,
to return from where never
before was true sovereignty.
The reach of the goddess: *Bride*'s bounds
to be set beseechingly, her Oyster-catchers
calling forth their ancient measures, newly inscribed.
Endlessly to mark and further mark
the limits of the land. Its regions:

its seven kingdoms under the cross to be one.
By token of the final marker. Alba
of the island and the entire island
and of the whole world, eventually.
Double-spun out of Northumbria:
here in imitation, in lost shadow,
but crucially. The strapwork
and the spiral. All the northern waters.
The insular style is one:
blended and unique, citing even Italy.

Saddles with stirrups, though foreseen by him,
along with several other contrivances,
were not authored by the Saviour.
Since, though instruments of good
and governmental guidance by God,

they have as direct a tendency to do evil
and do not quite belong in the historical pivot
allowed by the runes and carvings,
once quickly conveyed here from Greece
to recommence from the fastnesses.

He will establish his promise
towards his house, amongst the candidates
arraigned in white robes like the Romans,
where two or three suns appear
through a refraction of a cloud.
For though lychnobious creatures
delay, they yet assist the superterrestrials.
As enticing co-walkers they go before
and eventually outwork
the mocking and deluding entities.

And we may say here that the land
also arises, and that horizontal enchantments
do not after all stall the vertical dilation.
With the people surge likewise the waters;
with the sharp high ends last
equally the lingering pleasaunces.
Nor are the tripping darlings
to be cheated of their least quintessences.

Ascititious: the chosen, admitted,
associate or strange. Round
the *sith*'s hill dance the mountains
and round it rings the rising trees
and the twisted pathways
to a circular summit of an arboreal henge
older than any crafted stonework.

Tops of the pines, far away
from the earth, hold the heavens
at bay and their raging.
For us to walk endlessly
over innocuous needles,
in the lowest tier of a sheltered realm.
Skimming the floor,
we regard the many-barred silences,
the blue-hung intervals,
aspirate with a delay never for now
to be halted, though all
moss breathes 'eventually'.

The trees are the land's offering to the rain-shoots.
They receive their water yet shelter the
below-people from the deluge. Words hold
culture's ships at bay in the estuary,
just as things becalmed
dissipate continuance of green leafage.

Air torn invisibly by the screeches of seabirds
else healed with immediacy.
Perhaps punctuation of winds is its condition
of removal after untraceable disaster.
The birds awaken the atmosphere
by sounding their riffs to speak to us obscurely
of necessary patterns, unnoticed and unrealised.

Other flights list in floated languish to
the beating of their wing-dance,
unended, as of the earth-hall.

They heal and remind us
of a once great universal healing.

They soothe and recall us
to a calm reawakened life.

Silver rule by bells of the twinned sky and sea.
There are mountains behind the sun,
higher ever than the sun is or will be.
One glimpses them deeper-set than the sun's setting
in a dissolved mould,
from the vehicle's skimming of the low firth-bridge.
The sun's power is here fallen
and contained by the fern-leaves
and leaves of the bilberry.
Burning brown along the path to confine it
in all modesty while the silver sceptre sways
under the waning moon. To give the translucent grey
of the sea and sky that traces an arbitrary meridian
between the upper waters and the lower ones.

Spooling along their myriad crystal droplets.
Drenching us with briny striations.

On the cusp of Autumn:
the infinitely many crystal droplets.
They merge as one.
Manannan serves the Moon Goddess
and offers us music that discloses
the earth but is not of it,
to complete it and to mould
its glittering bridal archway to another world.

Its deviation being always secretly a portal,
since all roads are indirect,
the straight road after all curved like space
and the narrow way manifold.

So the infinitely many crystal droplets
merge as one lucidity, older than the sun,
more like the moon's echo of but one star.
To remind us that there are many,
but united in triple echo of the real one source,
rebound and acoustic. Thus the air makes
solidity sing, flow stay and burning warm.

And the infinitely diverse sparkling lights
that are the sea's trawl
penetrate each other to weave the filmy grey veil
that yields the antechamber of the hidden unity.

Eochar: key of the harvest.
Corn-stooks unfold in pale gold
before the blued-grey of the sea
as a time come, as lands in gift
of the wind that were not there before now.

Dalriada

Entranced by the stag to the dark wood,
the entangled wood,
the wood of mossy roots
stronger than stones.

The wood of dark coils,
of embossed, gleaming places,
the wood of stones
and the stones engreened.

Through your strayed lore
torn through the Dun's side
to the place of the *sidhe.*

Drawn to their sovereign darkness
by the first words
identifying darkness,
when I have shut away
– naming the perils –
my eyes to every image,
and my ears from every calling.

To list in order the old ones,
the heroes of Britain.
And first of all Arthur,
king of the islands.
Asleep now and dreaming
of the one remote island

and the woman there
clothed in the Sun's raiment.

On the mount of the way
of true words,
we shall not cease from rowing
till we have reached the island.

For to dwell in Britain,
to allow its secrets,
to assent to its hills that are all temples,
to its buildings that are all tombs,
is to search for its smallest volume.

And to be king here
is to leave the false claimants.

Is to leave the lures
of acceptable nuance in their candour
of fatal peace.

Is to seek always
for smaller islands,
for a power of condensation.
For many inlets
opening for all things
and by reduction
tracing a cosmos.

Until I-Thona:
wind and stones,
Carrog of the sea's heart
where they paint books perfect;
one book again, the one book
painted in the styles of the four peoples.

In the five tongues,
of which one, Gaelic,

was first from the tower compacted of many matters:
clay, wool, wood, blood, lime,
acacias, bitumen with virtue, water:
all nine that most remember
the first, fond mortar.

Before I go to face him
through the chariots of battle,
for the fitness of names
I bathe my palms
in showers of wine,
in the lustral fire,
in the juice of the rasps,
in the milk of honey
of the island of waves.

To the desert-isle
he took her: I-Thonn.
Druid isle: I-Thona.

Ending the claustrophobia of lochs
and the meaningless ruins of mountains
with their stark cold terrors
and slow cliffs,
as they slide, sickeningly and without import
towards the water.

Once withheld through so many twinings
and manifold craftwork of seduction –

these enlockings, escapings
of landscapes:
of Gaelic, Angle, Pictish, Brithonic;
of our being in battle by

tree-lore and dreaming,
by glory that records itself in dying,
when we sing of the conflict,
inspired by ghost-light.

For since the heroes
fought the unknown
alone, outside the Kingdom,
their most decisive history remains obscure,
except through their haunting
of poetic darkness.

So we shall not cease
from rowing till we reach
the noble island.

Where the woman
will dangle down her chain,
and men will be poured down,
poured like streams down
(at the waves' glen they too have rest).
Like streams down, poured out
as his work: saints
towards ladders for the city.

Excommunicate for fighting,
Columba left once, with his warband for the smallest island.
Still seeking her – *quiet* that shelters a wild hind,
she of the dark hair,
flying on the wave of the ocean,
her white breasts as snow
when the gentle winds rise
and slowly move it in the light.

She was pale, pale as the watery cloud.
For four days in a year they would mourn, daughters of Israel,
the daughter of Jeptha.
For four days,
with the return of the dark waters of Autumn.

She was like the fair spirit of heaven.
Her robe streamed in dusky wreaths.

Columba sought her;
he would be ruler.
And the King of Britain in his sleep,
In the oxter of the blue ocean
saw at last the flat rock of the roaring blue beast:
glass windows on it.

Fd: fedh ae, fundament
of clay, wool, wood, blood, lime,
acacias, bitumen with virtue, water.

And there are five forms of ae
that nourishes,

       sings,
       sues,
       judges,
       sits.

While for the hard root of names
we must graft from trees,
since the names of all trees
were ingredients at Babel.

On the mount of the way of true words,
your little hill;

on your right hand, O Son of God,
may I be at the day of doom.

She let down the black chain
for the sweet sorrow, singing
for him to reach,
to reach the land
where we expect Moses.

And he reached the plain
where they know the custom of music.
Sun-like exile, forever sailing.

You are the seed of the warrior host.
You are the seed of the tempestuous host.

My fragrant strong child,
he sought her.
Winsome her voice, stately her mien,
her white breast heaving
like the gull on the wave.

To her the darkness of night
is as the brightness of day, always.
From her *imbarla*
the pearl's birth
for which all is sold.

As a single kingdom
four kingdoms embarking
through the great obscurity,
grammatical darkness,
to set up the *bord cruinn,*
set it up with mirth and music.

Luis, Fern, Sail, Nin, Huath, Duir,
Tinne, Coll, Quiert, Muin, Gort, Ngetal,
Straiph, Ruis, Ailm, Onn, Ur, Edheadh,
Ido, Ebnadh, Oir, Uillead, Iphin.

Babel, Lot, Pharaoh, Saliath, Nebuchadnezzar,
Herod,
David, Talamon, Cae, Kahap, Muiriath, Goth,
Gomers, Strue, Ruben, Achab, Oise, Uirith,
Essu, Iachim, Ethrocius, Uimelicus,
Iudonius, Affrim, Ordines.

Lustre of eye	Shield of kings
Colour of death	A check on peace
Meet of Hounds	Higher than Bushes
Timber of chariot	Bearer of Nuts
Shelter of wild hind	Highest of berries
Binding of trees	Physician's strength
Hedge of a stream	Redness of shame
Shelter of death	The humble one
Trod underfoot	A grief extreme
The truest one	A grief again
More binding still.	

Near heaven upwards
with a roaring wind
the tower of Nimrod
falls to

Rowan, Alder, Willow,
Ash, Whitethorn, Oak,
Holly, Hazel, Apple,
Vine, Ivy, Fern,
Hedge, Elder, Fir-tree,

Furze, Heath, Aspen,
True-tree, Aspen-also, Spindle.

These twenty and more
persons, the noblest
of Fenian's school.

Not chiefless they have a house:
Tathus.
On darkness' path they have sense:
Tathus.

Sense. Sovereignty. A building. Order.

He crossed in ships the whales' shrine.
Not scant the thanks the birds gave.
On the mount of the way of true words
he will protect us in Sion.

Buried before aye, without recall.
Forsaking chariots, adoring boats.

Before I go to face him
through the panoply of battle
he has reached the land where night is not seen.

Following the love of the great King
for wisdom that urged the woman's law:
removing from battle the dark-haired one,
that we may war for her,
whose troop is radiant.

You, Columba of angelic beauty,
before the battle with Cadwallon,
were glimpsed by Oswald,

King of Northumbria,
dreaming from Lindisfarne to far Iona,

where the mountains part to the horizon,
to the sparkling,
even, infinite,
intimate to the distance,
entrancing sea

where the eye rests
when at the beyond-end she reaches.
It is a token of the soul's kinship,
boundless dilation.

On January's Nones,
at the difficult hour
of the cry of the host
from the dark wood,

grant me to write well,
birds of the world;
seeking from Columba's power,
power without ill,
by the wild-waved shores
of all the islands.

Whose long plunge
is to turquoise waves,
to a Pythagorean cone
of dusky sunbeams
and an emerald walk by a white wall
hidden far past the weeping wastes.

Within the *rath*,
after the *echtra*,

behold the *sidhe*.

After the misty journey
over the long plain,
the golden tree at the door,
with its roots here
and its flowers elsewhere.

The woman seated on her crystal chair
to offer the ale for the future King.

Within the *rath,*
your hill of angels,
where the war is.

I hear the voice on the wind
as the voice of the *ruach,*
seething fast through grasses
in the amber twilight:

'they did wonders in the morning
and at evening, but in the midday
lost their strength
and hid in holes in the ground'.

Their voice is lost, but only to Babel.
For we are a swirling pool,
lurking of browns, silver
with bog-myrtle, trailing marigolds.
Neither of Fingal nor of Arthur
may we know their earth,
for their renown is in their song
and as a dream to future times.

Yet she came,
Sovereignty,
Shekinah.

And we brightened in her presence
like a rock
before the sudden beams of the sun
when they issue from a barren cloud
divided by the roaring wind.

Notes on Sources, and Glossaries

TO THE WEST

Sources

Dryden, John, *An Ode on the Death of Mr Henry Purcell* [with musical score by John Blow] (London: Henry Playford, 1696).

DORSET SONG

Sources

Hardy, Thomas, *Far From the Madding Crowd* (Oxford: OUP, 1993).

'Whitchurch Canonicorum' in *Wikipedia* on the World Wide Web.

THE CHILDREN IN THE LAND OF SUMMER

Sources

Dryden, John, *'An Ode on the Death of Mr Henry Purcell'.*

Squire, Charles, *Celtic Myth and Legend: Poetry and Romance* (London: Gresham, 1923).

Dillon, Myles, *Early Irish Literature* (Black Rock, County Dublin: Four Courts Press, 1994).

Gantz, Jeffrey trans., *Early Irish Myths and Sagas* (London: Penguin, 1981).

The invocation here of echoes between Irish and British mythology and topography look forward to the final section and its inverse reference to a Gaelic-language account of the story of Arthur.

THE PEMBROKESHIRE COSMOLOGY

Primary Sources

Aneirin, *The Gododdin,* trans. Steve Short (Felinfach, Llanerch, 1994).

Geoffrey of Monmouth, *The History of the Kings of Britain,* trans. Lewis Thorpe (Harmondsworth: Penguin, 1966).

Glantz, Geoffrey trans. *The Mabinogion* (Harmondsworth: Penguin, 1976).

Gerald of Wales, *The Journey Through Wales/The Description of Wales,* trans. Lewis Thorpe (Harmondsworth: Penguin, 1978).

Pennar, Meirion trans. *The Black Book of Carmarthen* (Felinfach: Llanerch, 1989).

Williams, Ifor, *Armes Prydein: the Prophecy of Britain,* from *The Book of Taliesin* (Dublin: Dublin Institute for Advanced Studies, 1982).

[The poem includes direct citations from these sources.]

Secondary Sources
Charles-Edwards, T.M. *The Welsh Laws* (Cardiff: University of Wales Press, 1989).
Davies, Oliver, *Celtic Christianity in Early Medieval Wales* (Cardiff: University of Wales Press, 1996).
Allchin, A.M. *God's Presence Makes the World: the Celtic Vision Through the Centuries in Wales* (London: Darton, Longman and Todd, 1997).
Bryce, Derek, *Symbolism of the Celtic Cross* (Felinfach: Llanerch, 1994).

A Jutish Recounting

Sources
Johann Sebastian Bach, *Matthäus-Passion,* number 75, 'Mache dich, mein Herze, rein'.
St Augustine, *Enarrationes in Psalmos.*

This section of the poem is set on the Kentish coast during a wintry Easter. Kent was the ancient kingdom of the conquering Jutes and the territory upon which the first Christian missionaries from Rome later landed. 'Recounting' is intended as an equivalent of the Latin *enarratio* and these stanzas allude to the Augustinian theme of the *Vox Psalmos Totius Christi*: the voice of the psalms is the combined liturgical utterance of Christ as the head of the Church and the Church or the 'City of God in this world' as his body throughout history.

East Anglia

Aspects of the legend of the Norse/Saxon god Odin/Woden are here invoked.

The Trent *Aegir*

This section of the poem concerns the legend of the Danish-English king Cnut (Canute) and the waves. The river Trent flows in a curve from its source in the southern Pennines ('Peak District') northwards to the Humber estuary. In its final long stretch, where this section is set, it flows through the north-east Midlands county of Nottinghamshire.

The aegir is a tidal bore whose name may be derived from the sea-giant in Norse mythology.

THE HUNTING OF BARTLE

Sources

'Northern Traditions: The Burning of Bartle: West Witton in Wensleydale', and Andrew Bibby, 'Freedom to Roam: Wensleydale and Swaledale' on the World Wide Web.

Every August, on the Saturday nearest to St Bartholomew's day on the 24th, in the village of West Witton in Wensleydale in the North Riding of Yorkshire, an effigy called 'Bartle' is made by one of the Harker family and a song recounting the pursuit of the original 'Bartle' is chanted (till recently) by one of the Spencer family, as the figure is led in procession following the route of the chase from the height of Pen Hill above the village and then down the hillside into the centre of the village where 'Bartle' is finally burnt. There must be a connection with the fact that the parish church is dedicated to St Bartholomew and the proximity of the event to the saint's festival. Otherwise, the ceremony may commemorate the catching of a thief who stole sheep from the monks of Jervaulx Abbey nearby, and/or be linked to another local legend concerning the giant of Penwith.

NORTHUMBERLAND

Primary Sources

Bede, *A History of the English Church and People,* trans. Leo Shirley-Price (London: Penguin, 1975).

On the Measurement of Times trans. Faith Wallis (Liverpool: Liverpool University Press, 1999).

Mitchell, Bruce and Robinson, Fred C. eds. *Beowulf* (Oxford: Blackwell, 1998).

Secondary Sources

Hutton, Ronald, *The Pagan Religions of the Ancient British Isles: Their Nature and Legacy* (Blackwell: Oxford, 1998).

North, John, *Stonehenge* (London: Harper and Row, 1999).

GLOSSARY OF TECHNICAL TERMS

Gnomon	The upright indicator of a sundial.
Azimuth	A line on a horizontal.

Syzgia	Correspondence.
Dioptrae	Stakes aligned to the rising and setting sun in order to calculate equinoxes.

The Circhenn Medley

Sources

Gibbon, Lewis Grassic, *Sunset Song* (Edinburgh: Canongate, 2006).
Laing, Lloyd and Jenny, *The Picts and the Scots* (Stroud: Alan Sutton, 1993).

Circhenn, which now covers the areas of modern Angus and Kincardineshire (or 'The Mearns') in Eastern Scotland, was one of the seven provinces of ancient Pictland, and probably the most important.

Glossary of Scots words

Hirpling	Limping
Swithers	Agitations, hesitations.
Spurtle	A flat, wooden, spatula-like kitchen implement, used for turning oatcakes on a griddle.
Steering	Stirring.
Clairted	Smeared with dirt.

The Concealments of Buchan

Sources

Various legends pertaining to the castles of Delgatie, Fyvie and Huntly and to the wine tower in Fraserburgh are, in this section of the poem, promiscuously blended in a gothic mélange.

It is set in the county of Buchan on the Scottish East Coast, north of Aberdeen

Ethereal Banffshire

This part of the poem is set on the coast of Banffshire, west of Buchan in North East Scotland. It represents a degree zero of mythical invocation.

The Legacy of Alba

Primary Sources

Robert Kirk, *The Secret Commonwealth* and *A Short Treatise of the Scotish-Irish Charms and Spells* in *The Occult Laboratory: Magic, Science and Second Sight in Late 17th Century Scotland,* ed. Michael Hunter (Woodbridge: Boydell, 2001), 77-117.

Secondary Sources

Dauvit Broun, *Scottish Independence and the Idea of Britain: From the Picts to Alexander III* (Ednburgh: Edinburgh UP, 2007).

W.A. Cummins, *Decoding the Pictish Symbols* (Stroud, Glos: The History Press, 2009).

Stuart McHardy, *Pagan Symbols of the Picts* (Edinburgh: Luath, 2012).

F. Marian McNeill, *The Silver Bough* (Edinburgh: Canongate, 1989).

Alex Woolf, *From Pictland to Alba, 789-1070* (Edinburgh: Edinburgh UP, 2011).

This section of the poem is set in Sutherland, Caithness and the Central Highlands of Scotland.

Glossary of Scots and Gaelic Words

Sith   Fairies

Strath   A wide, shallow river valley (from Gaelic *srath*).

DALRIADA

Primary Sources

Adomnan of Iona, *Life of St Columba,* trans. Richard Sharpe (London: Penguin, 1995). See also Sharpe's introduction.

Calder, George, ed. *Auraicept Na N-Eces: The Scholar's Primer* (Blackrock, County Dublin: Four Courts Press, 1995).

Clancy, Thomas Owen and Markus, Gilbert, *Iona: The Earliest Poetry of a Celtic Monastery* (Edinburgh: Edinburgh UP, 1995).

Carmichael, Alexander, *Carmina Gaedelica: Hymns and Incantations* (Edinburgh: Floris, 1994).

Gowans, Linda, *An Bronn Binn: An Arthurian Ballad in Scottish Gaelic* (Eastbourne: Author-published, 1992).

Macpherson, James, *The Poems of Ossian and Related Works* ed. Howard Gaskill (Edinburgh: Edinburgh UP, 1996).

[The poem includes direct citations from these sources.]

Secondary Sources

Black, Ronald ed, *The Gaelic Otherworld* (Edinburgh: Berlinn, 2006) [A reprint of John Gregorson Campbell's *Superstitions of the Highlands and Islands of Scotland* and *Witchcraft and Second Sight in the Highlands and Islands* (Glasgow: James MacLehose, 1900/1902)]

Glennie, John R. Stuart, *Arthurian Localities: Their Historical Origin, Chief Country, and Fingalian Relations* (Felinfach: Llanerch, 1984). [Facsimile reprint of 1869 edition.]

Campbell, Ewan, 'Were the Scots Irish?' in *Antiquity* 75 (2001) 285-292.

'Dál Riata' in Wikipedia on the World Wide Web.

Laing, Lloyd and Jenny, *The Picts and the Scots*

Low, Mary, *Celtic Christianity and Nature: Early Irish and Hebridean Traditions* (Edinburgh: Edinburgh University Press 1996).

Marsden, John, *Sea-Road of the Saints: Celtic Holy Men in the Hebrides* (Edinburgh: Floris, 1995)

Tilley, Christopher, *A Phenomenology of Landscape: Places, Paths and Monuments* (Oxford: Berg, 1994).

Wainwright, F.T., *The Problem of the Picts* (London: Nelson, 1995).

Dalriada was a Gaelic overkingdom on the Western coast of Scotland, also comprising some territory on the northeastern coast of Ireland. These areas coincide roughly with modern Argyllshire (including the islands of Mull and Iona), Bute and Lochaber, together with County Antrim in Ulster. Although, according to mythical-chronological and Roman evidence, it would seem that this territory was conquered by Gaelic speakers from Ireland, recent archaeological evidence suggests that it was always a Goidelic rather than Brithonic-speaking Celtic area, and that it remained equally distinct in certain ways from most of Ireland both before and after later Irish incursions. In the 730s it was conquered by Pictish forces from Eastern Scotland, although the Pictish language later disappeared from the whole of Scotland when the Gaels seized the Pictish crown. It is now thought by some that the Pictish language may have been not purely Brithonic, but rather half-way between Brithonic or 'P' Celtic and Goidelic or 'Q' Celtic (as arguably reflected in many surviving place-names) and may even have been nearer to the latter than the former. The Q element would explain why the Pictish language was later so readily subsumed into Gaelic, while a continued influence of the P element may explain why Scottish Gaelic is slightly more similar to Welsh than is Irish Gaelic.

Glossary of Gaelic Words

Sidhe	Fairies.
Carrog	An artificial island constructed for dwelling in the midst of a lake.
Quiest	Apple-tree.
Imbarla	Esoteric knowledge; power to decipher cryptic language.
Bord Cruinn	Round-table.
Tathus	Sense and sovereignty.
Rath	Hill Fort; dwelling-place of fairies.
Echtra	Other-world journey.
Ruach (Hebrew)	Wind, breath, spirit.
Shekinah (Hebrew)	The female emanation and presence of God.

Lightning Source UK Ltd.
Milton Keynes UK
UKOW04f2255220215

246654UK00002B/22/P